School day

Monica Stoppleman

Photographs by Maggie Murray
Illustrations by Sheila Jackson

Contents

A & C Black · London

What's your school like?

Look at these two pictures. They show two schools in Nottingham. Your school probably looks like one of these. Which one would you say is the older? Which clues tell you about the age of the buildings? Is it their shape, their size, the material of which they're made, or a combination of these things?

One of these schools is built of bricks, and the other of reinforced concrete and painted wood. Look at the time-line on pages 6 and 7 to find out when builders first started using reinforced concrete.

What differences do you notice in the details on the buildings? Compare the decoration on the outside, the shape and style of the buildings.

Claremont Primary School, ▶ Nottingham. This school lies right on the road. At the back, behind a high wall, is a big asphalt yard.

Carrington Primary School, Nottingham. This school is set back from the road amongst trees and grass, with playing fields round the side.

Carrington School opened in 1964, when your parents were probably at school. Claremont School opened in 1884, when your great, great grandparents were children.

At the time when Claremont was being built, a huge number of new schools were opening all over the country. Before that there were very few proper school buildings. Teaching took place in churches, chapels, workshops or even under the arches of railway bridges!

The people who planned Carrington School were given plenty of land on which to build. They thought that as well as studying, children needed playing fields for sports. The planners of Claremont didn't have much land for their school, and they needed to fit in a lot of children. For them, learning to read, write, and do sums was the most important part of children's education. How do you think the planners' ideas influenced the way the schools were designed?

Inside your school now

Imagine you are showing your great, great grandparents round your school. Describe the kind of lessons you have and the equipment you use for writing, maths, craft work and gym. Tell them about the work pinned up on the walls and show them how many books there are.

How does your classroom compare with this one? Which things in it do you think will be unfamiliar to your visitor?

Class 10, Claremont Primary ▶ School. The children are working at low tables which can be moved around for other lessons. What activities can you see going on? Where is the teacher?

◀ At playtime, children are free to run around, buy snacks to eat and play whatever they choose. What are popular games at your school?

There are 27 children altogether in this class. They often work in groups. In this school, boys and girls sit together for lessons. At playtime, they sometimes prefer to play separately. At your school, are there any lessons or games that are just for boys or just for girls?

There are other grown-ups in schools as well as the teachers. Some of them do paid jobs, some of them are visitors and some come in from outside to do a job at the school. Find out who comes to your school and what they do.

Time-line

	pre-**1880s**	**1880s**	**1890s**	**1900s**	**1910s**	**1920**
		Great great grandparents were born		**Great grandparents were born**		

Important events

pre-**1880s**	**1880s**	**1890s**	**1900s**	**1910s**	**1920**
1870 Alexander Graham Bell invents telephone	**1888** Dunlop invents pneumatic tyre	**1890** Moving pictures start **1896** First modern Olympic Games	**1901** Queen Victoria dies. Edward VII becomes King **1903** Wright brothers fly first plane	**1910** George V becomes King **1914–18** World War I	**1920** Reinforce concrete common **1926** Gen Strike in Britain

School dates

pre-**1880s**	**1880s**	**1890s**	**1900s**	**1910s**	**1920**
1870 Education Act: School Boards set up, and all children must go to school until 10 years old ● $1\frac{1}{2}$ million children on school rolls 1 million attending **1870s** Huge increase in number of schools, private and state ● Most teachers aged between 13 and 18	**1880** School leaving age 13. Many 10–13 year olds work half-time	**1891** Elementary schooling made free in Board Schools. Private schools charge **1899** 'Special schools' set up for disabled children	**1901** $5\frac{1}{2}$ million children on school rolls, $4\frac{1}{2}$ million attending **1902** Local Education Authorities take over management of schools from School Boards ● First school nurses **1904** Government takes over organisation of secondary schooling **1906** Start of medical inspections of children **1907** Many schools have no drinking water, light or heating	**1908–11** School strikes all over England **1918** Half-time system abolished. School leaving age raised to 14 ● Employment of children under 12 is forbidden	**1928** Children's libraries n widesprea LIBRA

6

This time-line shows some of the important events since your great great grandparents were born and some of the events and inventions which have changed schools and lessons.

Grandparents were born		Parents were born		You were born		
1930s	**1940s**	**1950s**	**1960s**	**1970s**	**1980s**	**1990s**

1936 Edward VIII abdicates. George VI becomes King
● First television broadcasts

1939 World War II starts

1941 Penicillin successfully tested

1945 World War II ends

1947 First supersonic plane

1952 Elizabeth II becomes Queen

E II R

1959 Yuri Gagarin first man in space

1969 Neil Armstrong — first man on the moon

1973 Britain enters the Common Market

1981 First successful space shuttle flight

1934 Milk and meals free, on medical grounds, to 1 in 3 children

1940 Biro brothers patent the ballpoint pen
● School meals given as part of 'war economy'

1944 School leaving age for all children raised to 15
● Two main types of state school, grammar schools and secondary moderns. Children who fail the 11+ exam go to secondary moderns

1946 Free school milk for all children

1958 Government Act introduces comprehensive schools with no 11+ exam

1960 2 out of 3 children get free school dinners

1960s Computer studies begin in secondary schools
● Many children's school books now have colour pictures

1966 Most Local Education Authorities have 'gone comprehensive'

1973 School leaving age raised to 16

1980 Only a few children get free school dinners. Most bring sandwiches or pay in the cafeteria

1980s Computers used in primary schools

1988 Free school milk only for a few infants

1989 National Curriculum starts in schools. Testing of 7, 11 and 14 year-olds to be gradually introduced

This is Class 10 at Claremont Primary School. They wanted to find out who was at their school in great grandma's day. They borrowed the school's Admissions Register from their local Record Office and looked up the names and addresses of pupils who started school in 1904. Some of Class 10 found that there were pupils who had lived in their road, and even in their house!

Mr Rawson, who is now over 60, lent Class 10 a picture of his mother's class at their school in 1904. He said:

'That's my mother, Florrie Richards, on the top row. She was 8. George, her brother, is on the front row.'

▲ What differences can you see between the two class pictures? Which children look as though they are enjoying school?

▼ School Admissions Register, Carrington Boy's School, 1904.

Admission Number.	Date of Admission or Re-Admission.			Name in Full.	Name of Parent or Guardian.	Residence.	Whether exemption from Religious Instruction is claimed.	Date of Child's Birth.		
	Day.	Month.	Year.					Day.	Month.	Year.
2117	1	9	04	Limb, Edward	Limb, John	12 Winchester St.	No	2	10	95
2118	"	"	"	Franks, Arthur	Franks, Mary Ann	13 Glenroy Terrace, Hood St.	"	21	3	95
2119	"	"	"	Leaf, Frank	Leaf, George	36 Hood Street	"	16	3	95

8

▲ Children at the same school in 1904 – but this is only half the class! Can you spot Florrie and George?

▲ Mr Rawson's mother, Florrie, with the rest of her family.

Class 10 wondered why there were only white children in the picture, and were surprised to learn that there probably weren't any Afro-Caribbean or Asian children in Nottingham in 1904 (even though there were in other parts of the country). They tried to find out where their own great grandparents were then.

Only four children had great grandparents who lived in Nottingham. The others were in Spain, Poland, Germany, India, Jamaica, New Zealand or other parts of Britain.

Can you think who else is not in the picture? There are no children from wealthy families or even from modestly well-off homes: they were educated at home by a tutor or went to private schools. There are no children with physical or mental disabilities: they had a very limited education at special schools.

Inside school then

Class 10 searched the building for clues to tell them what school had been like in great grandma's day.

Plaques over the entrance of their school showed that boys and girls came in through separate doors. In the upstairs classrooms, the children found chimney breasts above where old fireplaces had been. The classrooms must have been heated by burning wood or coal.

▼ The bell tower, Claremont School. The bell is no longer in use. What do you think it was for?

▲ The school opened in 1884. There were three separate schools under one roof: Infants, Girls and Boys. They all came under one name: Carrington Schools. The school changed its name to Claremont Primary School in 1933. In 1964, the new primary school round the corner was opened and it took the old name, Carrington School.

The children noticed that dividing walls had been put up in some classrooms, so the classes had probably been much bigger then. They were puzzled by a trapdoor in the ceiling of the entrance hall. It was directly below the belltower. They guessed that this was where the rope for tolling the school bell used to hang.

The first state schools

Before the first state schools, School Board Visitors found that schools were few and many were squalid and over-crowded. ▶

◀ Over two million children didn't go to school. They had to work instead. These children were making match boxes in the 1890s. They worked about 14 hours a day, 6 days a week and earned two or three pence.

Before 1870, very few children went to school. Many had to start work when they were 6 or 7. But, in 1867, Parliament gave most men who owned or rented their homes the right to vote. Rich landowners complained that men who couldn't read or write had been given the power to decide who should run the country. So, in 1870, Parliament agreed that the children of 'the lower classes' should attend school and be taught to read and write.

All over the country, influential people were elected on to School Boards to organise this. The School Boards sent Visitors to find out what schools already existed.

11

Children started at the new Board Schools when they were five years old. They paid a few pence each week for their education. Some were kept away by their parents who couldn't afford to lose the money which their children earned. In 1891, Board Schools became free, to encourage more parents to send their children to them.

I can't do without my cheap nimble fingered workers! Why, I'll be ruined if I have to pay grown men's wages. Let 'em work hard at school till they're 10. Then they can come and learn an honest trade in my factory.

We can't do without our Arthur's wages. All we have to live on is £1 a week and a third of that goes on the rent. We'd be in the Workhouse without the two shillings he brings home.

My mother died last year, having our Mabel. There's no one else to look after the little 'uns. I've got to leave school now I'm 10.

Many employers also wanted children to continue working, so the School Boards agreed to a 'half-time system'. Children got up for work at 5 o'clock in the morning, then came to school, then went back to work till 10 o'clock at night. They were often too tired to learn.

The School Boards insisted that all headteachers kept a diary, or log, of school events. Class 10 looked at the Log Book for their school which covered the years 1883 to 1902. They found out that school started at 9 o'clock prompt. Children who didn't arrive on time were caned and their parents could be fined.

The school received a fixed amount of money from the School Board for each day a child attended. A low attendance meant less money to run the school. Some country schools relied on children bringing a lump of coal with them each day, to put on the stove.

▲ Some children had to walk three miles to and from school along unsurfaced roads and paths. When the weather was bad, schools had to close because the children couldn't get there. Children who came all year were rewarded with prizes, medals and certificates.

13

Great grandma's schoolroom, 1900

Some of the children in Class 10 visited a local museum, where they put on the sort of clothes that Florrie and George would have worn for school, and went into a classroom furnished as it would have been in 1900.

There was a high teacher's desk at the front of the class so that the teacher could see everyone. The children sat on benches, called forms, which were joined on to plank-like desks which had a shelf underneath. The desks were fixed to the floor and couldn't be moved. In great grandma's day, the children would not have been allowed to lean on their desks. They had to sit up straight all the time, scarcely ever moving from their place. Around eighty children would have sat squashed together in this classroom.

◄ This school in Northumberland had one classroom for its one hundred children.

This reconstructed classroom is at the Museum of Childhood, Sudbury Hall, Derbyshire. It contains desks and equipment which were used in local schools in great grandma's day.

The master or mistress was the only one who could move about freely, to write on the blackboard or to walk around the class checking on the children's work.

Mr Ainsworth, who went to school in 1908, remembered:

'He would ask you a question and if you got it wrong you had to move to the left, towards the bottom of the form, away from the stove that heated the room.'

Lessons

The youngest children started learning to write by drawing with their fingers in a tray of sand. Then they practised writing on a lined slate, with a slate pencil. In great grandma's day, good children used rags to clean their slates, but naughty ones used their hankies or 'spit and sleeve'. If the teacher caught them, they got the cane. Spitting was strictly forbidden; it was one of the ways that illnesses spread.

Older children wrote with pen and ink. Each week the teacher chose a child to be ink monitor, whose job was to hand out pens and mix ink. Pens were kept in a groove in the desk, so that they didn't roll off.

Class 10 tried to write on slates with slate pencils. They found it difficult to write without making a horrible squeaking noise.

16

It was considered very important for children to learn to write 'a fair hand' so that their writing would be easy to read. They learned by copying out sentences in copy books over and over again. They were only allowed to write with their right hand and carelessness was severely punished by caning.

Class 10 made some pens and tried to write in copperplate. The pens spattered and blotted and got clogged up. The children found it very difficult and decided they would probably have been given the cane in Florrie's day!

◀ The ink monitor handed out steel-nibbed pens, mixed the ink powder with water in a jug and poured it into inkwells. Before the invention of steel nibs, people used quill pens made from feathers.

▲ The children made penholders by cutting lengths of bamboo cane with a hacksaw. Then they made a hole in one end and pushed a nib into it.

Practising copperplate writing with a dip pen. ▶

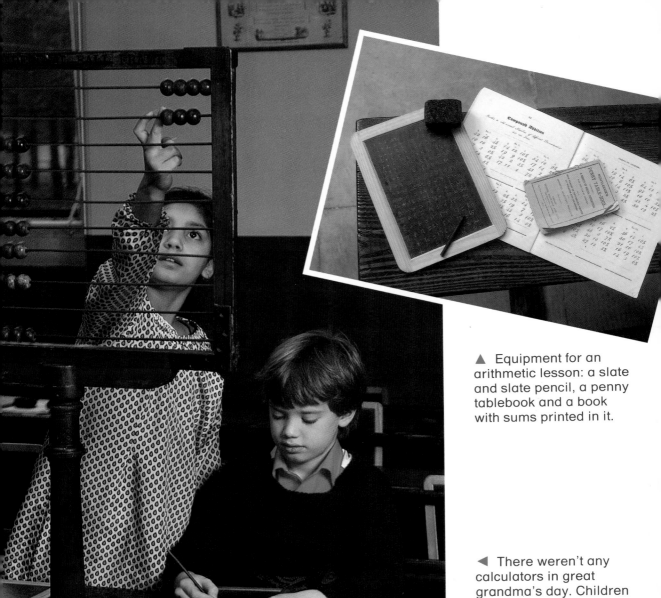

▲ Equipment for an arithmetic lesson: a slate and slate pencil, a penny tablebook and a book with sums printed in it.

◄ There weren't any calculators in great grandma's day. Children used an abacus to help them with their sums. The top row of beads represents units, the next row tens, the next row hundreds.

Young children learned their numbers by doing simple sums in their sand trays. Later, they wrote sums with hundreds, tens and units on slates, which were divided into squares. A great deal of time was spent chanting tables aloud.

Class libraries did not exist, and there were no books with colour photographs or illustrations. In many schools, there was only one reading book for the whole class. The children took it in turns to stand up, read and pass the book on. Mrs Ainsworth, who went to a Board School in 1906, said:

'This way of reading made even interesting stories dull, because it took so long to get through them.'

BROWNS' "ONWARD" TESTS.

FIRST YEAR
Card 13.

FIRST TERM.
1. Add twelve to seventeen.
2. If I can get 8 nuts for a farthing, how many can I get for 3 farthings?
3. Jack put eleven plums in the basket, and May put thirteen. How many was that?
4. How long is this line?

|_____|

5. 5 pears + 13 pears + 4 pears. How many pears?

SECOND TERM.
1. A girl buys a pound of butter for 1s. 4d., a dozen eggs for 9d., and a tin of meat for 10d. How much does she spend?
2. What shall I have left if I spend 9d. out of half-a-crown?
3. Draw a line 5½ inches long.
4. How many cards are there in 6 packets if there are 1 in each?
5. Find the total of 16 nuts + 17 nuts + 28 nuts.

THIRD TERM.
1. How much will 5 knives cost at 7½d. each?
2. If there are sixteen ounces in a pound, how many ounces make a quarter of a pound?
3. If I share 4s. 3d. among 6 boys, how much will each have?
4. Draw an oblong three inches long and half as wide as it is long.
5. A boy had 3 sixpences, 4 pennies, and five half-pennies. How much money had he?

A. BROWN & SONS, Ltd., LONDON, HULL and YORK.

FIRST INFANT READER.

1. KATE AND LILLY.

1. "It rains, it rains, it rains. Oh! how I wish it would give over," said Lilly to her sis-ter Kate. "I don't like it to rain when I want to go out to play.

2. "Do you think the rain does any good, Katie?"

3. "Oh! yes," said Kate. "The other day, when I was cross about the rain, mother said that God sent the rain as well as the sun-shine.

4. "If there were no rain we should have no water to drink, and all the birds and beasts would die of thirst, and so should we."

▲ A mental arithmetic card. Children of five would have been expected to be able to work out these sums in their heads.

◄ A primer for five year olds. Stories had strong moral messages.

19

On the blackboard:

Land and Water
Mountains Hills
cape Isthmus
Island
Ocean Sea River
Strait Bay Harbour

▲ A geography lesson in a London Board School, 1908.

sticky bud

tadpoles

snail shell

feather

nest

blackberries

conkers and acorns

Because there were so few books, lessons had to be learnt off by heart.

'In history we had to learn the names of all the kings and queens of England, and in geography we memorised all the rivers and mountains in Britain.'

Country children went out to collect flowers and leaves for nature study lessons. Most classrooms had a nature table with fossils and small skulls on it. Mrs Street, who went to a country school in 1906, remembered with pleasure:

'We'd go on a nature walk and take a milk can to get blackberries. By the time we got back, I'd ate all mine!'

The object lesson: the world in a box

An object box. ▶
The teacher selected one thing from it for the children to discuss. How many of these objects can you name?

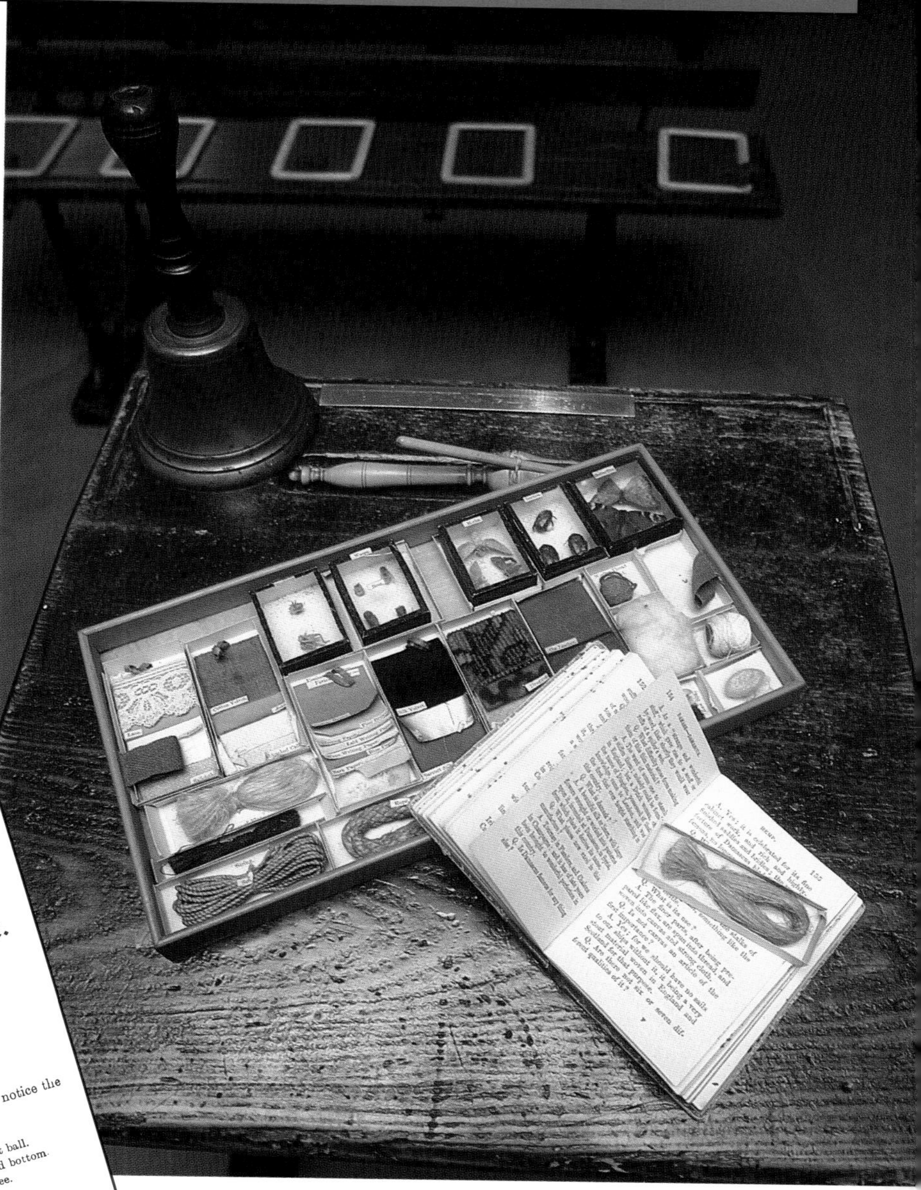

▼ A page taken from a guide for teachers on object lessons.

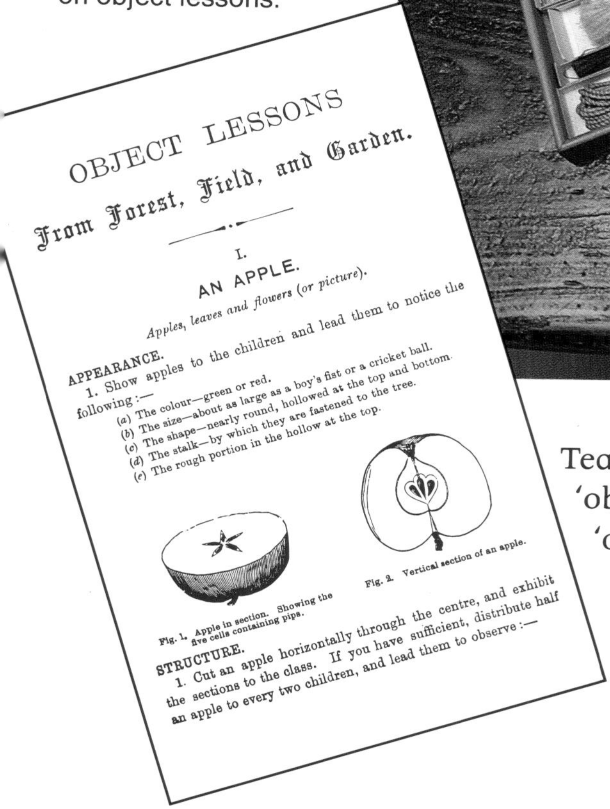

OBJECT LESSONS

From Forest, Field, and Garden.

I.

AN APPLE.

Apples, leaves and flowers (or picture).

APPEARANCE.

1. Show apples to the children and lead them to notice the following :—

(*a*) The colour—green or red.
(*b*) The size—about as large as a boy's fist or a cricket ball.
(*c*) The shape—nearly round, hollowed at the top and bottom.
(*d*) The stalk—by which they are fastened to the tree.
(*e*) The rough portion in the hollow at the top.

Fig. 1. Apple in section. Showing the five cells containing pips.

Fig. 2. Vertical section of an apple.

STRUCTURE.

1. Cut an apple horizontally through the centre, and exhibit the sections to the class. If you have sufficient, distribute half an apple to every two children, and lead them to observe :—

Teachers also kept a collection of things in an 'object box'. Once a week, they gave an 'object lesson'. Children had to look carefully at, for example, a lump of coal, a beetle or a piece of rope. They would have to draw and label it accurately and answer questions about it.

Different lessons for boys and girls

A woodwork lesson in 1908. ▶

▼ Girls sometimes went to the mistress' own house to practise housework.

People thought that boys and girls should learn different skills because when they left school they would do different jobs. The older boys were taught subjects which would help them in the building trade, heavy industry or agriculture. Only boys did drawing, which was considered a technical subject.

Girls were prepared for work in their own or other people's homes, and taught how to make clothes. By the time she left school, every girl was expected to be able to make a man's shirt by hand.

Mrs. Ainsworth remembered:

'We had to provide our own material for needlework. If girls couldn't, the headteacher bought the fabric. When the piece was finished, it was sold so that the money could be paid back. It was considered most important to learn not to be wasteful.'

Boys and girls did gym separately. It was called 'drill'. Schools had very little equipment, so drill was mainly a series of lifting and stretching exercises, done outside in the yard. The children had to follow the teacher's instructions exactly. Mrs Street, who went to the village school, said:

'We hated drill, especially when it was cold. In the winter we had to do it with our hats and coats on. The teachers didn't even get to move around, but had to stand at the front shouting instructions – so they liked it even less than us.'

▲ This girl is copying some Victorian stitching. Girls learnt to sew by practising basic stitches over and over again.

▼ Do girls wear clothes like this for exercising nowadays? Why not?

Learning on an empty belly

The Salvation Army provided Farthing Breakfasts for poor children. School dinners were started in 1941.

In great grandma's time many children went to school hungry, tired, and ill. Government reports at that time estimated that 1 in 3 children was half starved. Families simply could not afford to feed them properly. In towns, fresh food was very expensive. Meat was eaten once a week or less. Country children were usually better fed because their families often had a plot of land where they could grow vegetables and keep hens.

Make a list of what you had to eat yesterday. Compare it with this diet of a classmate of Florrie's. Children who lived too far away from school to go home to eat, brought a bottle of cold tea and a slice of bread or a potato in a hanky.

A day's food for a boy in a family of eight children. ▶
His father earned 30 shillings a week.

Bread and butter... BREAKFAST
tea

DINNER
Potatoes, greens, minced meat left over from the joint.

TEA
bread and jam
tea

When Board Schools were started, some people argued that meals should be provided by the schools. Others disagreed. Class 10 found this entry in their Logbook:

'Free meals would tend to pauperise the children and encourage the improvident.'

What do you think this meant?

The crowded stuffy classrooms were unhealthy places. Class 10 found entries about such diseases as mumps, measles, typhoid fever and diphtheria, which are now either unknown, or not very serious. In great grandma's day these were killers. Schools had to close for weeks to stop the spread of disease.

▲ This event is from the Carrington School Log Book in 1894. Quinsy was a severe throat infection. Visit your local cemetery to look for children's gravestones from around this time.

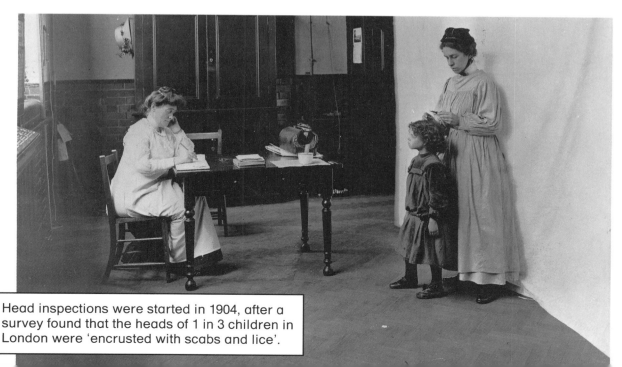

Head inspections were started in 1904, after a survey found that the heads of 1 in 3 children in London were 'encrusted with scabs and lice'.

25

Spare the rod and spoil the child

Classes were very large and teachers had difficulty keeping order. They often had to use physical force to control the children.

It wasn't unusual for parents to come into school to complain about their child being beaten – and many teachers were physically attacked by parents.

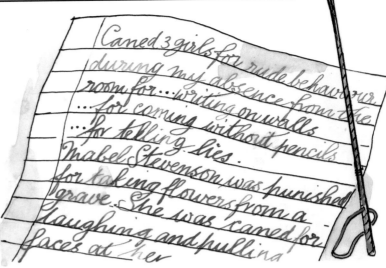

Caned 3 girls for rude behaviour during my absence from the room for... writing on walls ... for coming without pencils ... for telling lies. Mabel Stevenson was punished for taking flowers from a grave. She was caned for laughing and pulling faces at her

▼ Class 10 pretended to get the cane. It was hard for them to really imagine how a child in Florrie's time would have felt.

▲ Each beating with the cane or tawse (the Scottish name for the strap) had to be recorded in the logbook. But remember, this is the headteacher's version.

C D E F
I J K L

young minds.

your temper

to education

The teachers

Many of the teachers were hardly more than children themselves – aged between 13 and 18 years. Because there weren't enough qualified teachers, clever children were offered a tiny wage to stay on at school and pass on what they knew.

These pupil teachers worked alongside a qualified teacher, but many of them still found the work very difficult. They often had days off because of 'nervous headaches' and 'bilious attacks', and they caught all the children's illnesses.

After school, they had to prepare lessons and present them to the headteacher. This was called 'Criticism'. If they got favourable reports over five years, they could try for a place at one of the new training colleges.

▲ Starting in 1899 children, often backed by their parents, went on strike in some cities to demand an end to caning and excessive strictness. The biggest strikes were in 1911 and 1912. They made another demand: pocket money for going to school.

▼ Report in the Carrington Log on a pupil teacher in 1897. This sort of report by headteachers was common.

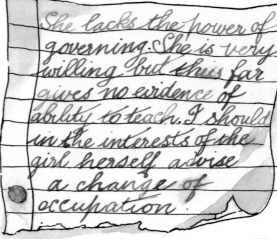

She lacks the power of governing. She is very willing but thus far gives no evidence of ability to teach. I should in the interests of the girl herself advise a change of occupation.

The inspectors

School Board inspectors went to schools regularly to see whether the teaching was up to standard. An inspector's visit was dreaded by everyone – especially as he never told anyone exactly what time he was coming.

Children who did not reach the required standard were not allowed to go up to the next class. For this reason, each class was called a 'Standard'. Some children never moved up from Standard 1. Those who did pass were given a certificate or a medal.

▼ A Merit Certificate. Each School Board had its own design. Some schools gave medals and ribbons.

The teachers made children repeat their lessons over and over again, so that they would be word perfect whenever the inspector turned up. Until 1890, schools were given extra money depending on how many children passed. But gradually, during the time that Florrie was at school, lessons began to be taught in a more interesting way.

West Bridgford C.E. School.

THIS IS TO CERTIFY

THAT

Clara Twelvetrees

WAS EXAMINED BY

HER MAJESTY'S INSPECTOR

and passed successfully in the 7th Standard on July 23rd, 1894.

Signed W. Stevenson, A.C.L.

Head Teacher

High days and holidays

Children dancing round the maypole, celebrating midsummer.

School wasn't all punishments and boring lessons. There were some enjoyable treats too: the Christmas concert, or the summer outing when the whole school and parents might go to the seaside. This was a very special occasion, and was all the holiday that most working people could hope for.

National events such as the monarch's birthday and Empire Day, when the children celebrated the British Empire, were also part of the school year. Privileges, such as riding in the procession, were used by teachers as rewards for good behaviour and regular attendance.

But, despite bribes and canings, there were some events that children always 'tipped off' for – haymaking in the country districts, the Fair, the Races. On these days many schools gave up and declared a holiday!

▲ A military display at Carrington School, 1906.

How to find out more

Start here	To find out about . . .	Who will have . . .
Old people	Their past	Memories, old photos, 'memorabilia' – things they've kept over the years, such as school books, certificates, medals
Libraries – public, in school, in local colleges	Books, archives, information about museums and local groups and resources such as local history society, oral history projects	● **Loan collections:** books to borrow ● **School loans service:** your teacher can borrow books for a term ● **Reference collections:** to use in the library. These may include back copies of magazines, newspapers, photographs of local people or buildings, tapes of people talking about their memories
Local museums	● School loans service ● Old objects, some quite large	● **Loan collections:** objects which schools can have for a whole term. They may be able to help you do a reconstruction in your classroom ● **Showcase displays:** irreplaceable objects, not for touching ● **Handling collections:** more robust items which you can examine ● **Reconstructions:** original objects from lots of different places put together to look like the real thing, the Victorian classroom ● **Reproductions:** Clothing or objects which have been made recently but look exactly like the original
Junk shops and flea markets	Old things	Smaller items, often slightly damaged, at reasonable prices – mugs, plates, clothes, pens, inkwells, old pictures
The Record Office, at the County Archives Department	Local documents. Photos	School log books, admissions registers, school plans, minutes of School Board meetings etc.

Who can tell you more?

They can! Ask if you may tape their stories, make a note of questions you want to ask. Label anything you are lent with name and date of loan, and arrange how to return it. Keep loans in a safe place

- The librarian

- Ask for the name of the secretary of the local history society for more local information

The education department, the loans officer. Your teacher will have to negotiate this

The museum curator or the education officer. Ask if they do special days when they give demonstrations

Go to your local museum first to get an idea of the kind of things to look out for

The archivist. Phone up to find out how to use their archives. Documents are largely for reference and cannot be taken away. However a school is entitled to borrow its own log book and admissions register, via the headteacher

Some useful addresses

The Museum of Childhood,
Sudbury Hall Sudbury DE6 5HT.
Tel: 028 378 305
Brewhouse Yard Museum
Nottingham.
Tel: 0602 483504
Herdings School Living History Centre
Norton Avenue, Sheffield 14.
Tel: 0742 653273
Scotland Street School
Glasgow.
Tel: 041 429 1202
Armley Mills Industrial Museum
Canal Rd, Armley,
Leeds LS12 2QF.
Old Grammar School,
South Church Side, Hull.
Tel: 0482 222737
The Old Village Primary School
Fringford, Oxfordshire
Tel: 0993 811456
The Ragged School Museum
46–48 Copperfield Rd. London E34 RR
Tel: 01–980–6405
The Museum of London
London Wall, London EC2Y 5NN
Tel: 01–600–3699
For information about your locality, contact the *Area Museum Service*, or look in the latest edition of *Museums and Art Galleries in Great Britain and Ireland* (British Leisure Publications).

A CIP catalogue record for this book is available from the British Library

ISBN 0–7136–3185–6

First published 1990 by A & C Black (Publishers) Ltd
35 Bedford Row, London WC1R 4JH

© 1990 A & C Black (Publishers) Ltd
Reprinted 1991, 1992

Filmset by August Filmsetting, Haydock, St Helens
Printed in Belgium by Proost International Book Production

Index

The author and publisher would like to thank all those who gave information and helped in the reconstruction of the classroom; David Bostock, Trevor Williams, Bill Belz, children and parents at Claremont Primary School.

They are also indebted to Mrs Payne at Carrington Primary School, the Administrator, the Education officer and the staff at the Derbyshire Museum of Childhood, Sudbury Hall; David Sorrell and staff at the Derbyshire County Museums Service; Mr Rawson; Mr and Mrs Ainsworth; Mrs Street; Mr Dawson and staff at Gedling House, Nottingham Schools Loan Service; Suella Postles at Brewhouse Yard Museum, Nottingham; Mrs Ford at Herdings Living History Centre.

Acknowledgements

Editor, Ruth Thomson

Photographs by Maggie Murray except for: p9 (top and bottom) Mr Rawson; p11 (top), 13, 14, 29 (top) Beamish Open Air Museum; p11 (bottom), 24 The Salvation Army; p13 (inset), 29 (bottom) Nottinghamshire County Library Archive Section; p19 Scotland Street School/Museum of Education; p20, 22 (top and bottom), 23, 25 Greater London Photographic Library; p27 The London Illustrated News Picture Library; Nottinghamshire Archives Office SBX 94/10. Reproduced by permission of the Principal Archivist
Cover (inset) Greater London Photographic Library